Collectibles
Record Keeper

A COLLECTOR'S COMPANION

by Vicki Fischer

PETER PAUPER PRESS, INC.
WHITE PLAINS, NEW YORK

The following images are used under license from Shutterstock.com
Cover © 2010 Andy Magee; © Design for Success
Front, back end paper © AKaiser; © 2010 Andy Magee;
© Liliya Kulianionak
p. 1 © Design for Success
p. 2 © Iakov Filimonov
p. 3 © Liliya Kulianionak; © Patricia Hofmeester
p. 4 © Liliya Kulianionak; © Brett Mulcahy;
© Tarasenko Sergey; © T.D.
p. 5 © Alice
p. 6 © Alice; © oknoart
p. 7 © Liliya Kulianionak; © KSPhotography;
© Elnur; © Sharon Day; © aquatic creature
p. 8 © Morozova Oxana
p. 139 © Liliya Kulianionak; © Gilmanshin © Margie Hurwich;
© joyfuldesigns; © Andreas Gradin; © Lana
p. 153 © Liliya Kulianionak; © Margo Harrison;
© Nicole Gordine; © Denise Kappa; © Pablo Romero

Designed by Heather Zschock

Copyright © 2011
Peter Pauper Press, Inc.
202 Mamaroneck Avenue
White Plains, NY 10601
All rights reserved

ISBN 978-1-4413-0574-9
Printed in Hong Kong
7 6 5 4 3 2 1

Collectibles

Record Keeper

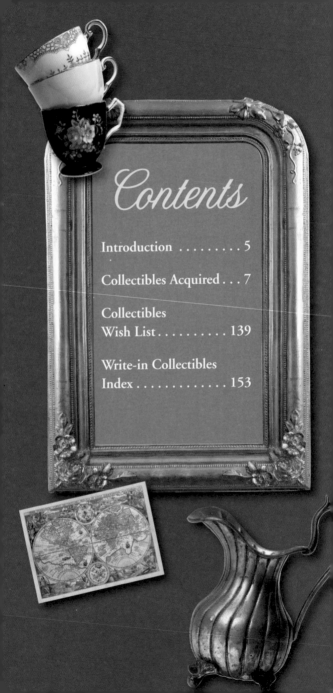

Contents

Introduction

Finally—a place to keep track of all your cherished collectibles, from retro salt and pepper shakers to irreplaceable family heirlooms, as well as things you've won on eBay, or found at flea markets, auctions, or tag sales.

- Use the **Collectibles Acquired** pages to note what you bought, including when, where, and for how much.

- **Wish List** pages keep you on task when it comes to building your collection.

- Write-in **Collectibles Index** pages at the back enable you to easily locate each item you've recorded.

- The convenient **back cover pocket** makes this record keeper extra useful.

Whether you collect *objets d'art* that are rare and difficult to find; kitschy, fun items like frog figurines or pink flamingos; or you're purchasing items for investment, here's just the *Collectibles Record Keeper* for you!

Track those treasures in an organized fashion as you record information about all your collectibles in one handy place, and build a valuable insurance record, too.

May this handy little volume enable you to organize your records and appreciate your collectibles, whether they be baseball cards, vintage jewelry, books, art, or anything else special to you.

Happy collecting!

COLLECTING IS LIKE EATING PEANUTS, YOU JUST CAN'T STOP.

AUTHOR UNKNOWN

Collectibles Acquired

Keep a record of your treasures—large and small— as you acquire them. Each collectible gets its own page for recording all the details of its discovery and transactions.

ITEM

DATE PURCHASED

VENDOR/STORE/DEALER

ADDRESS

PHONE #

WEB SITE/E-MAIL

ASKING PRICE   **PRICE PAID**

DESCRIPTION OF ITEM

YEAR ITEM WAS MADE

MANUFACTURER/ARTIST

MAKE/MODEL

CONDITION

ESTIMATED VALUE

WHERE STORED/KEPT

ADDITIONAL COMMENTS

ITEM

DATE PURCHASED

VENDOR/STORE/DEALER

ADDRESS

PHONE #

WEB SITE/E-MAIL

ASKING PRICE   **PRICE PAID**

DESCRIPTION OF ITEM

YEAR ITEM WAS MADE

MANUFACTURER/ARTIST

MAKE/MODEL

CONDITION

ESTIMATED VALUE

WHERE STORED/KEPT

ADDITIONAL COMMENTS

ITEM

DATE PURCHASED

VENDOR/STORE/DEALER

ADDRESS

PHONE #

WEB SITE/E-MAIL

ASKING PRICE   **PRICE PAID**

DESCRIPTION OF ITEM

YEAR ITEM WAS MADE

MANUFACTURER/ARTIST

MAKE/MODEL

CONDITION

ESTIMATED VALUE

WHERE STORED/KEPT

ADDITIONAL COMMENTS

ITEM

DATE PURCHASED

VENDOR/STORE/DEALER

ADDRESS

PHONE #

WEB SITE/E-MAIL

ASKING PRICE   **PRICE PAID**

DESCRIPTION OF ITEM

YEAR ITEM WAS MADE

MANUFACTURER/ARTIST

MAKE/MODEL

CONDITION

ESTIMATED VALUE

WHERE STORED/KEPT

ADDITIONAL COMMENTS

ITEM

DATE PURCHASED

VENDOR/STORE/DEALER

ADDRESS

PHONE #

WEB SITE/E-MAIL

ASKING PRICE   **PRICE PAID**

DESCRIPTION OF ITEM

YEAR ITEM WAS MADE

MANUFACTURER/ARTIST

MAKE/MODEL

CONDITION

ESTIMATED VALUE

WHERE STORED/KEPT

ADDITIONAL COMMENTS

ITEM

DATE PURCHASED

VENDOR/STORE/DEALER

ADDRESS

PHONE #

WEB SITE/E-MAIL

ASKING PRICE   **PRICE PAID**

DESCRIPTION OF ITEM

YEAR ITEM WAS MADE

MANUFACTURER/ARTIST

MAKE/MODEL

CONDITION

ESTIMATED VALUE

WHERE STORED/KEPT

ADDITIONAL COMMENTS

ITEM

DATE PURCHASED

VENDOR/STORE/DEALER

ADDRESS

PHONE #

WEB SITE/E-MAIL

ASKING PRICE   **PRICE PAID**

DESCRIPTION OF ITEM

YEAR ITEM WAS MADE

MANUFACTURER/ARTIST

MAKE/MODEL

CONDITION

ESTIMATED VALUE

WHERE STORED/KEPT

ADDITIONAL COMMENTS

ITEM

DATE PURCHASED

VENDOR/STORE/DEALER

ADDRESS

PHONE #

WEB SITE/E-MAIL

ASKING PRICE   **PRICE PAID**

DESCRIPTION OF ITEM

YEAR ITEM WAS MADE

MANUFACTURER/ARTIST

MAKE/MODEL

CONDITION

ESTIMATED VALUE

WHERE STORED/KEPT

ADDITIONAL COMMENTS

ITEM

DATE PURCHASED

VENDOR/STORE/DEALER

ADDRESS

PHONE #

WEB SITE/E-MAIL

ASKING PRICE   **PRICE PAID**

DESCRIPTION OF ITEM

YEAR ITEM WAS MADE

MANUFACTURER/ARTIST

MAKE/MODEL

CONDITION

ESTIMATED VALUE

WHERE STORED/KEPT

ADDITIONAL COMMENTS

ITEM

DATE PURCHASED

VENDOR/STORE/DEALER

ADDRESS

PHONE #

WEB SITE/E-MAIL

ASKING PRICE   **PRICE PAID**

DESCRIPTION OF ITEM

YEAR ITEM WAS MADE

MANUFACTURER/ARTIST

MAKE/MODEL

CONDITION

ESTIMATED VALUE

WHERE STORED/KEPT

ADDITIONAL COMMENTS

ITEM

DATE PURCHASED

VENDOR/STORE/DEALER

ADDRESS

PHONE #

WEB SITE/E-MAIL

ASKING PRICE **PRICE PAID**

DESCRIPTION OF ITEM

YEAR ITEM WAS MADE

MANUFACTURER/ARTIST

MAKE/MODEL

CONDITION

ESTIMATED VALUE

WHERE STORED/KEPT

ADDITIONAL COMMENTS

ITEM

DATE PURCHASED

VENDOR/STORE/DEALER

ADDRESS

PHONE #

WEB SITE/E-MAIL

ASKING PRICE　　　　　　**PRICE PAID**

DESCRIPTION OF ITEM

YEAR ITEM WAS MADE

MANUFACTURER/ARTIST

MAKE/MODEL

CONDITION

ESTIMATED VALUE

WHERE STORED/KEPT

ADDITIONAL COMMENTS

19

ITEM

DATE PURCHASED

VENDOR/STORE/DEALER

ADDRESS

PHONE #

WEB SITE/E-MAIL

ASKING PRICE   **PRICE PAID**

DESCRIPTION OF ITEM

YEAR ITEM WAS MADE

MANUFACTURER/ARTIST

MAKE/MODEL

CONDITION

ESTIMATED VALUE

WHERE STORED/KEPT

ADDITIONAL COMMENTS

ITEM

DATE PURCHASED

VENDOR/STORE/DEALER

ADDRESS

PHONE #

WEB SITE/E-MAIL

ASKING PRICE   **PRICE PAID**

DESCRIPTION OF ITEM

YEAR ITEM WAS MADE

MANUFACTURER/ARTIST

MAKE/MODEL

CONDITION

ESTIMATED VALUE

WHERE STORED/KEPT

ADDITIONAL COMMENTS

ITEM

DATE PURCHASED

VENDOR/STORE/DEALER

ADDRESS

PHONE #

WEB SITE/E-MAIL

ASKING PRICE   **PRICE PAID**

DESCRIPTION OF ITEM

YEAR ITEM WAS MADE

MANUFACTURER/ARTIST

MAKE/MODEL

CONDITION

ESTIMATED VALUE

WHERE STORED/KEPT

ADDITIONAL COMMENTS

ITEM

DATE PURCHASED

VENDOR/STORE/DEALER

ADDRESS

PHONE #

WEB SITE/E-MAIL

ASKING PRICE   **PRICE PAID**

DESCRIPTION OF ITEM

YEAR ITEM WAS MADE

MANUFACTURER/ARTIST

MAKE/MODEL

CONDITION

ESTIMATED VALUE

WHERE STORED/KEPT

ADDITIONAL COMMENTS

ITEM

DATE PURCHASED

VENDOR/STORE/DEALER

ADDRESS

PHONE #

WEB SITE/E-MAIL

ASKING PRICE   **PRICE PAID**

DESCRIPTION OF ITEM

YEAR ITEM WAS MADE

MANUFACTURER/ARTIST

MAKE/MODEL

CONDITION

ESTIMATED VALUE

WHERE STORED/KEPT

ADDITIONAL COMMENTS

ITEM

DATE PURCHASED

VENDOR/STORE/DEALER

ADDRESS

PHONE #

WEB SITE/E-MAIL

ASKING PRICE   **PRICE PAID**

DESCRIPTION OF ITEM

YEAR ITEM WAS MADE

MANUFACTURER/ARTIST

MAKE/MODEL

CONDITION

ESTIMATED VALUE

WHERE STORED/KEPT

ADDITIONAL COMMENTS

ITEM

DATE PURCHASED

VENDOR/STORE/DEALER

ADDRESS

PHONE #

WEB SITE/E-MAIL

ASKING PRICE   **PRICE PAID**

DESCRIPTION OF ITEM

YEAR ITEM WAS MADE

MANUFACTURER/ARTIST

MAKE/MODEL

CONDITION

ESTIMATED VALUE

WHERE STORED/KEPT

ADDITIONAL COMMENTS

ITEM

DATE PURCHASED

VENDOR/STORE/DEALER

ADDRESS

PHONE #

WEB SITE/E-MAIL

ASKING PRICE　　　　　　　**PRICE PAID**

DESCRIPTION OF ITEM

YEAR ITEM WAS MADE

MANUFACTURER/ARTIST

MAKE/MODEL

CONDITION

ESTIMATED VALUE

WHERE STORED/KEPT

ADDITIONAL COMMENTS

ITEM

DATE PURCHASED

VENDOR/STORE/DEALER

ADDRESS

PHONE #

WEB SITE/E-MAIL

ASKING PRICE   **PRICE PAID**

DESCRIPTION OF ITEM

YEAR ITEM WAS MADE

MANUFACTURER/ARTIST

MAKE/MODEL

CONDITION

ESTIMATED VALUE

WHERE STORED/KEPT

ADDITIONAL COMMENTS

ITEM

DATE PURCHASED

VENDOR/STORE/DEALER

ADDRESS

PHONE #

WEB SITE/E-MAIL

ASKING PRICE   **PRICE PAID**

DESCRIPTION OF ITEM

YEAR ITEM WAS MADE

MANUFACTURER/ARTIST

MAKE/MODEL

CONDITION

ESTIMATED VALUE

WHERE STORED/KEPT

ADDITIONAL COMMENTS

ITEM

DATE PURCHASED

VENDOR/STORE/DEALER

ADDRESS

PHONE #

WEB SITE/E-MAIL

ASKING PRICE   **PRICE PAID**

DESCRIPTION OF ITEM

YEAR ITEM WAS MADE

MANUFACTURER/ARTIST

MAKE/MODEL

CONDITION

ESTIMATED VALUE

WHERE STORED/KEPT

ADDITIONAL COMMENTS

ITEM

DATE PURCHASED

VENDOR/STORE/DEALER

ADDRESS

PHONE #

WEB SITE/E-MAIL

ASKING PRICE   **PRICE PAID**

DESCRIPTION OF ITEM

YEAR ITEM WAS MADE

MANUFACTURER/ARTIST

MAKE/MODEL

CONDITION

ESTIMATED VALUE

WHERE STORED/KEPT

ADDITIONAL COMMENTS

ITEM

DATE PURCHASED

VENDOR/STORE/DEALER

ADDRESS

PHONE #

WEB SITE/E-MAIL

ASKING PRICE   **PRICE PAID**

DESCRIPTION OF ITEM

YEAR ITEM WAS MADE

MANUFACTURER/ARTIST

MAKE/MODEL

CONDITION

ESTIMATED VALUE

WHERE STORED/KEPT

ADDITIONAL COMMENTS

ITEM

DATE PURCHASED

VENDOR/STORE/DEALER

ADDRESS

PHONE #

WEB SITE/E-MAIL

ASKING PRICE　　　　　　　　**PRICE PAID**

DESCRIPTION OF ITEM

YEAR ITEM WAS MADE

MANUFACTURER/ARTIST

MAKE/MODEL

CONDITION

ESTIMATED VALUE

WHERE STORED/KEPT

ADDITIONAL COMMENTS

ITEM

DATE PURCHASED

VENDOR/STORE/DEALER

ADDRESS

PHONE #

WEB SITE/E-MAIL

ASKING PRICE   **PRICE PAID**

DESCRIPTION OF ITEM

YEAR ITEM WAS MADE

MANUFACTURER/ARTIST

MAKE/MODEL

CONDITION

ESTIMATED VALUE

WHERE STORED/KEPT

ADDITIONAL COMMENTS

ITEM

DATE PURCHASED

VENDOR/STORE/DEALER

ADDRESS

PHONE #

WEB SITE/E-MAIL

ASKING PRICE   **PRICE PAID**

DESCRIPTION OF ITEM

YEAR ITEM WAS MADE

MANUFACTURER/ARTIST

MAKE/MODEL

CONDITION

ESTIMATED VALUE

WHERE STORED/KEPT

ADDITIONAL COMMENTS

ITEM

DATE PURCHASED

VENDOR/STORE/DEALER

ADDRESS

PHONE #

WEB SITE/E-MAIL

ASKING PRICE   **PRICE PAID**

DESCRIPTION OF ITEM

YEAR ITEM WAS MADE

MANUFACTURER/ARTIST

MAKE/MODEL

CONDITION

ESTIMATED VALUE

WHERE STORED/KEPT

ADDITIONAL COMMENTS

ITEM

DATE PURCHASED

VENDOR/STORE/DEALER

ADDRESS

PHONE #

WEB SITE/E-MAIL

ASKING PRICE   **PRICE PAID**

DESCRIPTION OF ITEM

YEAR ITEM WAS MADE

MANUFACTURER/ARTIST

MAKE/MODEL

CONDITION

ESTIMATED VALUE

WHERE STORED/KEPT

ADDITIONAL COMMENTS

ITEM

DATE PURCHASED

VENDOR/STORE/DEALER

ADDRESS

PHONE #

WEB SITE/E-MAIL

ASKING PRICE   **PRICE PAID**

DESCRIPTION OF ITEM

YEAR ITEM WAS MADE

MANUFACTURER/ARTIST

MAKE/MODEL

CONDITION

ESTIMATED VALUE

WHERE STORED/KEPT

ADDITIONAL COMMENTS

ITEM

DATE PURCHASED

VENDOR/STORE/DEALER

ADDRESS

PHONE #

WEB SITE/E-MAIL

ASKING PRICE   **PRICE PAID**

DESCRIPTION OF ITEM

YEAR ITEM WAS MADE

MANUFACTURER/ARTIST

MAKE/MODEL

CONDITION

ESTIMATED VALUE

WHERE STORED/KEPT

ADDITIONAL COMMENTS

ITEM

DATE PURCHASED

VENDOR/STORE/DEALER

ADDRESS

PHONE #

WEB SITE/E-MAIL

ASKING PRICE   **PRICE PAID**

DESCRIPTION OF ITEM

YEAR ITEM WAS MADE

MANUFACTURER/ARTIST

MAKE/MODEL

CONDITION

ESTIMATED VALUE

WHERE STORED/KEPT

ADDITIONAL COMMENTS

ITEM

DATE PURCHASED

VENDOR/STORE/DEALER

ADDRESS

PHONE #

WEB SITE/E-MAIL

ASKING PRICE   **PRICE PAID**

DESCRIPTION OF ITEM

YEAR ITEM WAS MADE

MANUFACTURER/ARTIST

MAKE/MODEL

CONDITION

ESTIMATED VALUE

WHERE STORED/KEPT

ADDITIONAL COMMENTS

41

ITEM

DATE PURCHASED

VENDOR/STORE/DEALER

ADDRESS

PHONE #

WEB SITE/E-MAIL

ASKING PRICE   **PRICE PAID**

DESCRIPTION OF ITEM

YEAR ITEM WAS MADE

MANUFACTURER/ARTIST

MAKE/MODEL

CONDITION

ESTIMATED VALUE

WHERE STORED/KEPT

ADDITIONAL COMMENTS

ITEM

DATE PURCHASED

VENDOR/STORE/DEALER

ADDRESS

PHONE #

WEB SITE/E-MAIL

ASKING PRICE   **PRICE PAID**

DESCRIPTION OF ITEM

YEAR ITEM WAS MADE

MANUFACTURER/ARTIST

MAKE/MODEL

CONDITION

ESTIMATED VALUE

WHERE STORED/KEPT

ADDITIONAL COMMENTS

ITEM

DATE PURCHASED

VENDOR/STORE/DEALER

ADDRESS

PHONE #

WEB SITE/E-MAIL

ASKING PRICE   **PRICE PAID**

DESCRIPTION OF ITEM

YEAR ITEM WAS MADE

MANUFACTURER/ARTIST

MAKE/MODEL

CONDITION

ESTIMATED VALUE

WHERE STORED/KEPT

ADDITIONAL COMMENTS

ITEM

DATE PURCHASED

VENDOR/STORE/DEALER

ADDRESS

PHONE #

WEB SITE/E-MAIL

ASKING PRICE　　　　　　　　**PRICE PAID**

DESCRIPTION OF ITEM

YEAR ITEM WAS MADE

MANUFACTURER/ARTIST

MAKE/MODEL

CONDITION

ESTIMATED VALUE

WHERE STORED/KEPT

ADDITIONAL COMMENTS

ITEM

DATE PURCHASED

VENDOR/STORE/DEALER

ADDRESS

PHONE #

WEB SITE/E-MAIL

ASKING PRICE   **PRICE PAID**

DESCRIPTION OF ITEM

YEAR ITEM WAS MADE

MANUFACTURER/ARTIST

MAKE/MODEL

CONDITION

ESTIMATED VALUE

WHERE STORED/KEPT

ADDITIONAL COMMENTS

ITEM

DATE PURCHASED

VENDOR/STORE/DEALER

ADDRESS

PHONE #

WEB SITE/E-MAIL

ASKING PRICE   **PRICE PAID**

DESCRIPTION OF ITEM

YEAR ITEM WAS MADE

MANUFACTURER/ARTIST

MAKE/MODEL

CONDITION

ESTIMATED VALUE

WHERE STORED/KEPT

ADDITIONAL COMMENTS

ITEM

DATE PURCHASED

VENDOR/STORE/DEALER

ADDRESS

PHONE #

WEB SITE/E-MAIL

ASKING PRICE   **PRICE PAID**

DESCRIPTION OF ITEM

YEAR ITEM WAS MADE

MANUFACTURER/ARTIST

MAKE/MODEL

CONDITION

ESTIMATED VALUE

WHERE STORED/KEPT

ADDITIONAL COMMENTS

ITEM

DATE PURCHASED

VENDOR/STORE/DEALER

ADDRESS

PHONE #

WEB SITE/E-MAIL

ASKING PRICE   **PRICE PAID**

DESCRIPTION OF ITEM

YEAR ITEM WAS MADE

MANUFACTURER/ARTIST

MAKE/MODEL

CONDITION

ESTIMATED VALUE

WHERE STORED/KEPT

ADDITIONAL COMMENTS

ITEM

DATE PURCHASED

VENDOR/STORE/DEALER

ADDRESS

PHONE #

WEB SITE/E-MAIL

ASKING PRICE   **PRICE PAID**

DESCRIPTION OF ITEM

YEAR ITEM WAS MADE

MANUFACTURER/ARTIST

MAKE/MODEL

CONDITION

ESTIMATED VALUE

WHERE STORED/KEPT

ADDITIONAL COMMENTS

ITEM

DATE PURCHASED

VENDOR/STORE/DEALER

ADDRESS

PHONE #

WEB SITE/E-MAIL

ASKING PRICE   **PRICE PAID**

DESCRIPTION OF ITEM

YEAR ITEM WAS MADE

MANUFACTURER/ARTIST

MAKE/MODEL

CONDITION

ESTIMATED VALUE

WHERE STORED/KEPT

ADDITIONAL COMMENTS

ITEM

DATE PURCHASED

VENDOR/STORE/DEALER

ADDRESS

PHONE #

WEB SITE/E-MAIL

ASKING PRICE　　　　　　**PRICE PAID**

DESCRIPTION OF ITEM

YEAR ITEM WAS MADE

MANUFACTURER/ARTIST

MAKE/MODEL

CONDITION

ESTIMATED VALUE

WHERE STORED/KEPT

ADDITIONAL COMMENTS

52

ITEM

DATE PURCHASED

VENDOR/STORE/DEALER

ADDRESS

PHONE #

WEB SITE/E-MAIL

ASKING PRICE   **PRICE PAID**

DESCRIPTION OF ITEM

YEAR ITEM WAS MADE

MANUFACTURER/ARTIST

MAKE/MODEL

CONDITION

ESTIMATED VALUE

WHERE STORED/KEPT

ADDITIONAL COMMENTS

ITEM

DATE PURCHASED

VENDOR/STORE/DEALER

ADDRESS

PHONE #

WEB SITE/E-MAIL

ASKING PRICE   **PRICE PAID**

DESCRIPTION OF ITEM

YEAR ITEM WAS MADE

MANUFACTURER/ARTIST

MAKE/MODEL

CONDITION

ESTIMATED VALUE

WHERE STORED/KEPT

ADDITIONAL COMMENTS

ITEM

DATE PURCHASED

VENDOR/STORE/DEALER

ADDRESS

PHONE #

WEB SITE/E-MAIL

ASKING PRICE   **PRICE PAID**

DESCRIPTION OF ITEM

YEAR ITEM WAS MADE

MANUFACTURER/ARTIST

MAKE/MODEL

CONDITION

ESTIMATED VALUE

WHERE STORED/KEPT

ADDITIONAL COMMENTS

ITEM

DATE PURCHASED

VENDOR/STORE/DEALER

ADDRESS

PHONE #

WEB SITE/E-MAIL

ASKING PRICE   **PRICE PAID**

DESCRIPTION OF ITEM

YEAR ITEM WAS MADE

MANUFACTURER/ARTIST

MAKE/MODEL

CONDITION

ESTIMATED VALUE

WHERE STORED/KEPT

ADDITIONAL COMMENTS

ITEM

DATE PURCHASED

VENDOR/STORE/DEALER

ADDRESS

PHONE #

WEB SITE/E-MAIL

ASKING PRICE   **PRICE PAID**

DESCRIPTION OF ITEM

YEAR ITEM WAS MADE

MANUFACTURER/ARTIST

MAKE/MODEL

CONDITION

ESTIMATED VALUE

WHERE STORED/KEPT

ADDITIONAL COMMENTS

ITEM

DATE PURCHASED

VENDOR/STORE/DEALER

ADDRESS

PHONE #

WEB SITE/E-MAIL

ASKING PRICE   **PRICE PAID**

DESCRIPTION OF ITEM

YEAR ITEM WAS MADE

MANUFACTURER/ARTIST

MAKE/MODEL

CONDITION

ESTIMATED VALUE

WHERE STORED/KEPT

ADDITIONAL COMMENTS

ITEM

DATE PURCHASED

VENDOR/STORE/DEALER

ADDRESS

PHONE #

WEB SITE/E-MAIL

ASKING PRICE   **PRICE PAID**

DESCRIPTION OF ITEM

YEAR ITEM WAS MADE

MANUFACTURER/ARTIST

MAKE/MODEL

CONDITION

ESTIMATED VALUE

WHERE STORED/KEPT

ADDITIONAL COMMENTS

ITEM

DATE PURCHASED

VENDOR/STORE/DEALER

ADDRESS

PHONE #

WEB SITE/E-MAIL

ASKING PRICE   **PRICE PAID**

DESCRIPTION OF ITEM

YEAR ITEM WAS MADE

MANUFACTURER/ARTIST

MAKE/MODEL

CONDITION

ESTIMATED VALUE

WHERE STORED/KEPT

ADDITIONAL COMMENTS

ITEM

DATE PURCHASED

VENDOR/STORE/DEALER

ADDRESS

PHONE #

WEB SITE/E-MAIL

ASKING PRICE   **PRICE PAID**

DESCRIPTION OF ITEM

YEAR ITEM WAS MADE

MANUFACTURER/ARTIST

MAKE/MODEL

CONDITION

ESTIMATED VALUE

WHERE STORED/KEPT

ADDITIONAL COMMENTS

ITEM

DATE PURCHASED

VENDOR/STORE/DEALER

ADDRESS

PHONE #

WEB SITE/E-MAIL

ASKING PRICE   **PRICE PAID**

DESCRIPTION OF ITEM

YEAR ITEM WAS MADE

MANUFACTURER/ARTIST

MAKE/MODEL

CONDITION

ESTIMATED VALUE

WHERE STORED/KEPT

ADDITIONAL COMMENTS

ITEM

DATE PURCHASED

VENDOR/STORE/DEALER

ADDRESS

PHONE #

WEB SITE/E-MAIL

ASKING PRICE   **PRICE PAID**

DESCRIPTION OF ITEM

YEAR ITEM WAS MADE

MANUFACTURER/ARTIST

MAKE/MODEL

CONDITION

ESTIMATED VALUE

WHERE STORED/KEPT

ADDITIONAL COMMENTS

ITEM

DATE PURCHASED

VENDOR/STORE/DEALER

ADDRESS

PHONE #

WEB SITE/E-MAIL

ASKING PRICE   **PRICE PAID**

DESCRIPTION OF ITEM

YEAR ITEM WAS MADE

MANUFACTURER/ARTIST

MAKE/MODEL

CONDITION

ESTIMATED VALUE

WHERE STORED/KEPT

ADDITIONAL COMMENTS

ITEM

DATE PURCHASED

VENDOR/STORE/DEALER

ADDRESS

PHONE #

WEB SITE/E-MAIL

ASKING PRICE   **PRICE PAID**

DESCRIPTION OF ITEM

YEAR ITEM WAS MADE

MANUFACTURER/ARTIST

MAKE/MODEL

CONDITION

ESTIMATED VALUE

WHERE STORED/KEPT

ADDITIONAL COMMENTS

ITEM

DATE PURCHASED

VENDOR/STORE/DEALER

ADDRESS

PHONE #

WEB SITE/E-MAIL

ASKING PRICE   **PRICE PAID**

DESCRIPTION OF ITEM

YEAR ITEM WAS MADE

MANUFACTURER/ARTIST

MAKE/MODEL

CONDITION

ESTIMATED VALUE

WHERE STORED/KEPT

ADDITIONAL COMMENTS

ITEM

DATE PURCHASED

VENDOR/STORE/DEALER

ADDRESS

PHONE #

WEB SITE/E-MAIL

ASKING PRICE   **PRICE PAID**

DESCRIPTION OF ITEM

YEAR ITEM WAS MADE

MANUFACTURER/ARTIST

MAKE/MODEL

CONDITION

ESTIMATED VALUE

WHERE STORED/KEPT

ADDITIONAL COMMENTS

ITEM

DATE PURCHASED

VENDOR/STORE/DEALER

ADDRESS

PHONE #

WEB SITE/E-MAIL

ASKING PRICE   **PRICE PAID**

DESCRIPTION OF ITEM

YEAR ITEM WAS MADE

MANUFACTURER/ARTIST

MAKE/MODEL

CONDITION

ESTIMATED VALUE

WHERE STORED/KEPT

ADDITIONAL COMMENTS

ITEM

DATE PURCHASED

VENDOR/STORE/DEALER

ADDRESS

PHONE #

WEB SITE/E-MAIL

ASKING PRICE   **PRICE PAID**

DESCRIPTION OF ITEM

YEAR ITEM WAS MADE

MANUFACTURER/ARTIST

MAKE/MODEL

CONDITION

ESTIMATED VALUE

WHERE STORED/KEPT

ADDITIONAL COMMENTS

ITEM

DATE PURCHASED

VENDOR/STORE/DEALER

ADDRESS

PHONE #

WEB SITE/E-MAIL

ASKING PRICE   **PRICE PAID**

DESCRIPTION OF ITEM

YEAR ITEM WAS MADE

MANUFACTURER/ARTIST

MAKE/MODEL

CONDITION

ESTIMATED VALUE

WHERE STORED/KEPT

ADDITIONAL COMMENTS

ITEM

DATE PURCHASED

VENDOR/STORE/DEALER

ADDRESS

PHONE #

WEB SITE/E-MAIL

ASKING PRICE   **PRICE PAID**

DESCRIPTION OF ITEM

YEAR ITEM WAS MADE

MANUFACTURER/ARTIST

MAKE/MODEL

CONDITION

ESTIMATED VALUE

WHERE STORED/KEPT

ADDITIONAL COMMENTS

ITEM

DATE PURCHASED

VENDOR/STORE/DEALER

ADDRESS

PHONE #

WEB SITE/E-MAIL

ASKING PRICE **PRICE PAID**

DESCRIPTION OF ITEM

YEAR ITEM WAS MADE

MANUFACTURER/ARTIST

MAKE/MODEL

CONDITION

ESTIMATED VALUE

WHERE STORED/KEPT

ADDITIONAL COMMENTS

ITEM

DATE PURCHASED

VENDOR/STORE/DEALER

ADDRESS

PHONE #

WEB SITE/E-MAIL

ASKING PRICE   **PRICE PAID**

DESCRIPTION OF ITEM

YEAR ITEM WAS MADE

MANUFACTURER/ARTIST

MAKE/MODEL

CONDITION

ESTIMATED VALUE

WHERE STORED/KEPT

ADDITIONAL COMMENTS

ITEM

DATE PURCHASED

VENDOR/STORE/DEALER

ADDRESS

PHONE #

WEB SITE/E-MAIL

ASKING PRICE   **PRICE PAID**

DESCRIPTION OF ITEM

YEAR ITEM WAS MADE

MANUFACTURER/ARTIST

MAKE/MODEL

CONDITION

ESTIMATED VALUE

WHERE STORED/KEPT

ADDITIONAL COMMENTS

ITEM

DATE PURCHASED

VENDOR/STORE/DEALER

ADDRESS

PHONE #

WEB SITE/E-MAIL

ASKING PRICE   **PRICE PAID**

DESCRIPTION OF ITEM

YEAR ITEM WAS MADE

MANUFACTURER/ARTIST

MAKE/MODEL

CONDITION

ESTIMATED VALUE

WHERE STORED/KEPT

ADDITIONAL COMMENTS

ITEM

DATE PURCHASED

VENDOR/STORE/DEALER

ADDRESS

PHONE #

WEB SITE/E-MAIL

ASKING PRICE   **PRICE PAID**

DESCRIPTION OF ITEM

YEAR ITEM WAS MADE

MANUFACTURER/ARTIST

MAKE/MODEL

CONDITION

ESTIMATED VALUE

WHERE STORED/KEPT

ADDITIONAL COMMENTS

ITEM

DATE PURCHASED

VENDOR/STORE/DEALER

ADDRESS

PHONE #

WEB SITE/E-MAIL

ASKING PRICE   **PRICE PAID**

DESCRIPTION OF ITEM

YEAR ITEM WAS MADE

MANUFACTURER/ARTIST

MAKE/MODEL

CONDITION

ESTIMATED VALUE

WHERE STORED/KEPT

ADDITIONAL COMMENTS

ITEM

DATE PURCHASED

VENDOR/STORE/DEALER

ADDRESS

PHONE #

WEB SITE/E-MAIL

ASKING PRICE　　　　　　**PRICE PAID**

DESCRIPTION OF ITEM

YEAR ITEM WAS MADE

MANUFACTURER/ARTIST

MAKE/MODEL

CONDITION

ESTIMATED VALUE

WHERE STORED/KEPT

ADDITIONAL COMMENTS

ITEM

DATE PURCHASED

VENDOR/STORE/DEALER

ADDRESS

PHONE #

WEB SITE/E-MAIL

ASKING PRICE   **PRICE PAID**

DESCRIPTION OF ITEM

YEAR ITEM WAS MADE

MANUFACTURER/ARTIST

MAKE/MODEL

CONDITION

ESTIMATED VALUE

WHERE STORED/KEPT

ADDITIONAL COMMENTS

ITEM

DATE PURCHASED

VENDOR/STORE/DEALER

ADDRESS

PHONE #

WEB SITE/E-MAIL

ASKING PRICE   **PRICE PAID**

DESCRIPTION OF ITEM

YEAR ITEM WAS MADE

MANUFACTURER/ARTIST

MAKE/MODEL

CONDITION

ESTIMATED VALUE

WHERE STORED/KEPT

ADDITIONAL COMMENTS

ITEM

DATE PURCHASED

VENDOR/STORE/DEALER

ADDRESS

PHONE #

WEB SITE/E-MAIL

ASKING PRICE   **PRICE PAID**

DESCRIPTION OF ITEM

YEAR ITEM WAS MADE

MANUFACTURER/ARTIST

MAKE/MODEL

CONDITION

ESTIMATED VALUE

WHERE STORED/KEPT

ADDITIONAL COMMENTS

ITEM

DATE PURCHASED

VENDOR/STORE/DEALER

ADDRESS

PHONE #

WEB SITE/E-MAIL

ASKING PRICE   **PRICE PAID**

DESCRIPTION OF ITEM

YEAR ITEM WAS MADE

MANUFACTURER/ARTIST

MAKE/MODEL

CONDITION

ESTIMATED VALUE

WHERE STORED/KEPT

ADDITIONAL COMMENTS

ITEM

DATE PURCHASED

VENDOR/STORE/DEALER

ADDRESS

PHONE #

WEB SITE/E-MAIL

ASKING PRICE   **PRICE PAID**

DESCRIPTION OF ITEM

YEAR ITEM WAS MADE

MANUFACTURER/ARTIST

MAKE/MODEL

CONDITION

ESTIMATED VALUE

WHERE STORED/KEPT

ADDITIONAL COMMENTS

ITEM

DATE PURCHASED

VENDOR/STORE/DEALER

ADDRESS

PHONE #

WEB SITE/E-MAIL

ASKING PRICE   **PRICE PAID**

DESCRIPTION OF ITEM

YEAR ITEM WAS MADE

MANUFACTURER/ARTIST

MAKE/MODEL

CONDITION

ESTIMATED VALUE

WHERE STORED/KEPT

ADDITIONAL COMMENTS

ITEM

DATE PURCHASED

VENDOR/STORE/DEALER

ADDRESS

PHONE #

WEB SITE/E-MAIL

ASKING PRICE　　　　　　　　**PRICE PAID**

DESCRIPTION OF ITEM

YEAR ITEM WAS MADE

MANUFACTURER/ARTIST

MAKE/MODEL

CONDITION

ESTIMATED VALUE

WHERE STORED/KEPT

ADDITIONAL COMMENTS

ITEM

DATE PURCHASED

VENDOR/STORE/DEALER

ADDRESS

PHONE #

WEB SITE/E-MAIL

ASKING PRICE　　　　　　**PRICE PAID**

DESCRIPTION OF ITEM

YEAR ITEM WAS MADE

MANUFACTURER/ARTIST

MAKE/MODEL

CONDITION

ESTIMATED VALUE

WHERE STORED/KEPT

ADDITIONAL COMMENTS

86

ITEM

DATE PURCHASED

VENDOR/STORE/DEALER

ADDRESS

PHONE #

WEB SITE/E-MAIL

ASKING PRICE   **PRICE PAID**

DESCRIPTION OF ITEM

YEAR ITEM WAS MADE

MANUFACTURER/ARTIST

MAKE/MODEL

CONDITION

ESTIMATED VALUE

WHERE STORED/KEPT

ADDITIONAL COMMENTS

ITEM

DATE PURCHASED

VENDOR/STORE/DEALER

ADDRESS

PHONE #

WEB SITE/E-MAIL

ASKING PRICE   **PRICE PAID**

DESCRIPTION OF ITEM

YEAR ITEM WAS MADE

MANUFACTURER/ARTIST

MAKE/MODEL

CONDITION

ESTIMATED VALUE

WHERE STORED/KEPT

ADDITIONAL COMMENTS

ITEM

DATE PURCHASED

VENDOR/STORE/DEALER

ADDRESS

PHONE #

WEB SITE/E-MAIL

ASKING PRICE   **PRICE PAID**

DESCRIPTION OF ITEM

YEAR ITEM WAS MADE

MANUFACTURER/ARTIST

MAKE/MODEL

CONDITION

ESTIMATED VALUE

WHERE STORED/KEPT

ADDITIONAL COMMENTS

ITEM

DATE PURCHASED

VENDOR/STORE/DEALER

ADDRESS

PHONE #

WEB SITE/E-MAIL

ASKING PRICE   **PRICE PAID**

DESCRIPTION OF ITEM

YEAR ITEM WAS MADE

MANUFACTURER/ARTIST

MAKE/MODEL

CONDITION

ESTIMATED VALUE

WHERE STORED/KEPT

ADDITIONAL COMMENTS

ITEM

DATE PURCHASED

VENDOR/STORE/DEALER

ADDRESS

PHONE #

WEB SITE/E-MAIL

ASKING PRICE   **PRICE PAID**

DESCRIPTION OF ITEM

YEAR ITEM WAS MADE

MANUFACTURER/ARTIST

MAKE/MODEL

CONDITION

ESTIMATED VALUE

WHERE STORED/KEPT

ADDITIONAL COMMENTS

ITEM

DATE PURCHASED

VENDOR/STORE/DEALER

ADDRESS

PHONE #

WEB SITE/E-MAIL

ASKING PRICE   **PRICE PAID**

DESCRIPTION OF ITEM

YEAR ITEM WAS MADE

MANUFACTURER/ARTIST

MAKE/MODEL

CONDITION

ESTIMATED VALUE

WHERE STORED/KEPT

ADDITIONAL COMMENTS

ITEM

DATE PURCHASED

VENDOR/STORE/DEALER

ADDRESS

PHONE #

WEB SITE/E-MAIL

ASKING PRICE   **PRICE PAID**

DESCRIPTION OF ITEM

YEAR ITEM WAS MADE

MANUFACTURER/ARTIST

MAKE/MODEL

CONDITION

ESTIMATED VALUE

WHERE STORED/KEPT

ADDITIONAL COMMENTS

ITEM

DATE PURCHASED

VENDOR/STORE/DEALER

ADDRESS

PHONE #

WEB SITE/E-MAIL

ASKING PRICE   **PRICE PAID**

DESCRIPTION OF ITEM

YEAR ITEM WAS MADE

MANUFACTURER/ARTIST

MAKE/MODEL

CONDITION

ESTIMATED VALUE

WHERE STORED/KEPT

ADDITIONAL COMMENTS

ITEM

DATE PURCHASED

VENDOR/STORE/DEALER

ADDRESS

PHONE #

WEB SITE/E-MAIL

ASKING PRICE   **PRICE PAID**

DESCRIPTION OF ITEM

YEAR ITEM WAS MADE

MANUFACTURER/ARTIST

MAKE/MODEL   .

CONDITION

ESTIMATED VALUE

WHERE STORED/KEPT

ADDITIONAL COMMENTS

ITEM

DATE PURCHASED

VENDOR/STORE/DEALER

ADDRESS

PHONE #

WEB SITE/E-MAIL

ASKING PRICE   **PRICE PAID**

DESCRIPTION OF ITEM

YEAR ITEM WAS MADE

MANUFACTURER/ARTIST

MAKE/MODEL

CONDITION

ESTIMATED VALUE

WHERE STORED/KEPT

ADDITIONAL COMMENTS

ITEM

DATE PURCHASED

VENDOR/STORE/DEALER

ADDRESS

PHONE #

WEB SITE/E-MAIL

ASKING PRICE   **PRICE PAID**

DESCRIPTION OF ITEM

YEAR ITEM WAS MADE

MANUFACTURER/ARTIST

MAKE/MODEL

CONDITION

ESTIMATED VALUE

WHERE STORED/KEPT

ADDITIONAL COMMENTS

ITEM

DATE PURCHASED

VENDOR/STORE/DEALER

ADDRESS

PHONE #

WEB SITE/E-MAIL

ASKING PRICE   **PRICE PAID**

DESCRIPTION OF ITEM

YEAR ITEM WAS MADE

MANUFACTURER/ARTIST

MAKE/MODEL

CONDITION

ESTIMATED VALUE

WHERE STORED/KEPT

ADDITIONAL COMMENTS

ITEM

DATE PURCHASED

VENDOR/STORE/DEALER

ADDRESS

PHONE #

WEB SITE/E-MAIL

ASKING PRICE   **PRICE PAID**

DESCRIPTION OF ITEM

YEAR ITEM WAS MADE

MANUFACTURER/ARTIST

MAKE/MODEL

CONDITION

ESTIMATED VALUE

WHERE STORED/KEPT

ADDITIONAL COMMENTS

ITEM

DATE PURCHASED

VENDOR/STORE/DEALER

ADDRESS

PHONE #

WEB SITE/E-MAIL

ASKING PRICE   **PRICE PAID**

DESCRIPTION OF ITEM

YEAR ITEM WAS MADE

MANUFACTURER/ARTIST

MAKE/MODEL

CONDITION

ESTIMATED VALUE

WHERE STORED/KEPT

ADDITIONAL COMMENTS

ITEM

DATE PURCHASED

VENDOR/STORE/DEALER

ADDRESS

PHONE #

WEB SITE/E-MAIL

ASKING PRICE   **PRICE PAID**

DESCRIPTION OF ITEM

YEAR ITEM WAS MADE

MANUFACTURER/ARTIST

MAKE/MODEL

CONDITION

ESTIMATED VALUE

WHERE STORED/KEPT

ADDITIONAL COMMENTS

ITEM

DATE PURCHASED

VENDOR/STORE/DEALER

ADDRESS

PHONE #

WEB SITE/E-MAIL

ASKING PRICE   **PRICE PAID**

DESCRIPTION OF ITEM

YEAR ITEM WAS MADE

MANUFACTURER/ARTIST

MAKE/MODEL

CONDITION

ESTIMATED VALUE

WHERE STORED/KEPT

ADDITIONAL COMMENTS

ITEM

DATE PURCHASED

VENDOR/STORE/DEALER

ADDRESS

PHONE #

WEB SITE/E-MAIL

ASKING PRICE   **PRICE PAID**

DESCRIPTION OF ITEM

YEAR ITEM WAS MADE

MANUFACTURER/ARTIST

MAKE/MODEL

CONDITION

ESTIMATED VALUE

WHERE STORED/KEPT

ADDITIONAL COMMENTS

ITEM

DATE PURCHASED

VENDOR/STORE/DEALER

ADDRESS

PHONE #

WEB SITE/E-MAIL

ASKING PRICE   **PRICE PAID**

DESCRIPTION OF ITEM

YEAR ITEM WAS MADE

MANUFACTURER/ARTIST

MAKE/MODEL

CONDITION

ESTIMATED VALUE

WHERE STORED/KEPT

ADDITIONAL COMMENTS

ITEM

DATE PURCHASED

VENDOR/STORE/DEALER

ADDRESS

PHONE #

WEB SITE/E-MAIL

ASKING PRICE   **PRICE PAID**

DESCRIPTION OF ITEM

YEAR ITEM WAS MADE

MANUFACTURER/ARTIST

MAKE/MODEL

CONDITION

ESTIMATED VALUE

WHERE STORED/KEPT

ADDITIONAL COMMENTS

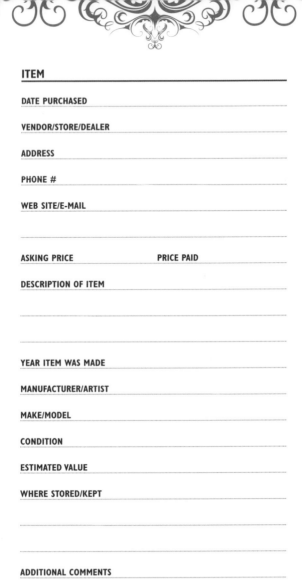

ITEM

DATE PURCHASED

VENDOR/STORE/DEALER

ADDRESS

PHONE #

WEB SITE/E-MAIL

ASKING PRICE   **PRICE PAID**

DESCRIPTION OF ITEM

YEAR ITEM WAS MADE

MANUFACTURER/ARTIST

MAKE/MODEL

CONDITION

ESTIMATED VALUE

WHERE STORED/KEPT

ADDITIONAL COMMENTS

ITEM

DATE PURCHASED

VENDOR/STORE/DEALER

ADDRESS

PHONE #

WEB SITE/E-MAIL

ASKING PRICE   **PRICE PAID**

DESCRIPTION OF ITEM

YEAR ITEM WAS MADE

MANUFACTURER/ARTIST

MAKE/MODEL

CONDITION

ESTIMATED VALUE

WHERE STORED/KEPT

ADDITIONAL COMMENTS

ITEM

DATE PURCHASED

VENDOR/STORE/DEALER

ADDRESS

PHONE #

WEB SITE/E-MAIL

ASKING PRICE   **PRICE PAID**

DESCRIPTION OF ITEM

YEAR ITEM WAS MADE

MANUFACTURER/ARTIST

MAKE/MODEL

CONDITION

ESTIMATED VALUE

WHERE STORED/KEPT

ADDITIONAL COMMENTS

ITEM

DATE PURCHASED

VENDOR/STORE/DEALER

ADDRESS

PHONE #

WEB SITE/E-MAIL

ASKING PRICE   **PRICE PAID**

DESCRIPTION OF ITEM

YEAR ITEM WAS MADE

MANUFACTURER/ARTIST

MAKE/MODEL

CONDITION

ESTIMATED VALUE

WHERE STORED/KEPT

ADDITIONAL COMMENTS

ITEM

DATE PURCHASED

VENDOR/STORE/DEALER

ADDRESS

PHONE #

WEB SITE/E-MAIL

ASKING PRICE   **PRICE PAID**

DESCRIPTION OF ITEM

YEAR ITEM WAS MADE

MANUFACTURER/ARTIST

MAKE/MODEL

CONDITION

ESTIMATED VALUE

WHERE STORED/KEPT

ADDITIONAL COMMENTS

ITEM

DATE PURCHASED

VENDOR/STORE/DEALER

ADDRESS

PHONE #

WEB SITE/E-MAIL

ASKING PRICE   **PRICE PAID**

DESCRIPTION OF ITEM

YEAR ITEM WAS MADE

MANUFACTURER/ARTIST

MAKE/MODEL

CONDITION

ESTIMATED VALUE

WHERE STORED/KEPT

ADDITIONAL COMMENTS

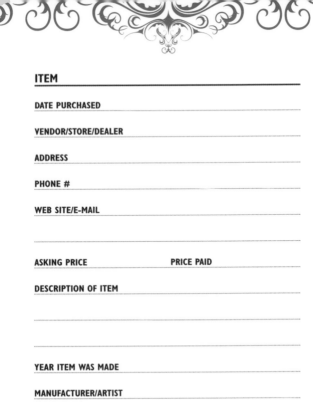

ITEM

DATE PURCHASED

VENDOR/STORE/DEALER

ADDRESS

PHONE #

WEB SITE/E-MAIL

ASKING PRICE   **PRICE PAID**

DESCRIPTION OF ITEM

YEAR ITEM WAS MADE

MANUFACTURER/ARTIST

MAKE/MODEL

CONDITION

ESTIMATED VALUE

WHERE STORED/KEPT

ADDITIONAL COMMENTS

ITEM

DATE PURCHASED

VENDOR/STORE/DEALER

ADDRESS

PHONE #

WEB SITE/E-MAIL

ASKING PRICE   **PRICE PAID**

DESCRIPTION OF ITEM

YEAR ITEM WAS MADE

MANUFACTURER/ARTIST

MAKE/MODEL

CONDITION

ESTIMATED VALUE

WHERE STORED/KEPT

ADDITIONAL COMMENTS

ITEM

DATE PURCHASED

VENDOR/STORE/DEALER

ADDRESS

PHONE #

WEB SITE/E-MAIL

ASKING PRICE   **PRICE PAID**

DESCRIPTION OF ITEM

YEAR ITEM WAS MADE

MANUFACTURER/ARTIST

MAKE/MODEL

CONDITION

ESTIMATED VALUE

WHERE STORED/KEPT

ADDITIONAL COMMENTS

ITEM

DATE PURCHASED

VENDOR/STORE/DEALER

ADDRESS

PHONE #

WEB SITE/E-MAIL

ASKING PRICE   **PRICE PAID**

DESCRIPTION OF ITEM

YEAR ITEM WAS MADE

MANUFACTURER/ARTIST

MAKE/MODEL

CONDITION

ESTIMATED VALUE

WHERE STORED/KEPT

ADDITIONAL COMMENTS

ITEM

DATE PURCHASED

VENDOR/STORE/DEALER

ADDRESS

PHONE #

WEB SITE/E-MAIL

ASKING PRICE   **PRICE PAID**

DESCRIPTION OF ITEM

YEAR ITEM WAS MADE

MANUFACTURER/ARTIST

MAKE/MODEL

CONDITION

ESTIMATED VALUE

WHERE STORED/KEPT

ADDITIONAL COMMENTS

ITEM

DATE PURCHASED

VENDOR/STORE/DEALER

ADDRESS

PHONE #

WEB SITE/E-MAIL

ASKING PRICE   **PRICE PAID**

DESCRIPTION OF ITEM

YEAR ITEM WAS MADE

MANUFACTURER/ARTIST

MAKE/MODEL

CONDITION

ESTIMATED VALUE

WHERE STORED/KEPT

ADDITIONAL COMMENTS

ITEM

DATE PURCHASED

VENDOR/STORE/DEALER

ADDRESS

PHONE #

WEB SITE/E-MAIL

ASKING PRICE   **PRICE PAID**

DESCRIPTION OF ITEM

YEAR ITEM WAS MADE

MANUFACTURER/ARTIST

MAKE/MODEL

CONDITION

ESTIMATED VALUE

WHERE STORED/KEPT

ADDITIONAL COMMENTS

ITEM

DATE PURCHASED

VENDOR/STORE/DEALER

ADDRESS

PHONE #

WEB SITE/E-MAIL

ASKING PRICE　　　　　　**PRICE PAID**

DESCRIPTION OF ITEM

YEAR ITEM WAS MADE

MANUFACTURER/ARTIST

MAKE/MODEL

CONDITION

ESTIMATED VALUE

WHERE STORED/KEPT

ADDITIONAL COMMENTS

ITEM

DATE PURCHASED

VENDOR/STORE/DEALER

ADDRESS

PHONE #

WEB SITE/E-MAIL

ASKING PRICE　　　　　　**PRICE PAID**

DESCRIPTION OF ITEM

YEAR ITEM WAS MADE

MANUFACTURER/ARTIST

MAKE/MODEL

CONDITION

ESTIMATED VALUE

WHERE STORED/KEPT

ADDITIONAL COMMENTS

120

ITEM

DATE PURCHASED

VENDOR/STORE/DEALER

ADDRESS

PHONE #

WEB SITE/E-MAIL

ASKING PRICE   **PRICE PAID**

DESCRIPTION OF ITEM

YEAR ITEM WAS MADE

MANUFACTURER/ARTIST

MAKE/MODEL

CONDITION

ESTIMATED VALUE

WHERE STORED/KEPT

ADDITIONAL COMMENTS

ITEM

DATE PURCHASED

VENDOR/STORE/DEALER

ADDRESS

PHONE #

WEB SITE/E-MAIL

ASKING PRICE   **PRICE PAID**

DESCRIPTION OF ITEM

YEAR ITEM WAS MADE

MANUFACTURER/ARTIST

MAKE/MODEL

CONDITION

ESTIMATED VALUE

WHERE STORED/KEPT

ADDITIONAL COMMENTS

ITEM

DATE PURCHASED

VENDOR/STORE/DEALER

ADDRESS

PHONE #

WEB SITE/E-MAIL

ASKING PRICE   **PRICE PAID**

DESCRIPTION OF ITEM

YEAR ITEM WAS MADE

MANUFACTURER/ARTIST

MAKE/MODEL

CONDITION

ESTIMATED VALUE

WHERE STORED/KEPT

ADDITIONAL COMMENTS

ITEM

DATE PURCHASED

VENDOR/STORE/DEALER

ADDRESS

PHONE #

WEB SITE/E-MAIL

ASKING PRICE   **PRICE PAID**

DESCRIPTION OF ITEM

YEAR ITEM WAS MADE

MANUFACTURER/ARTIST

MAKE/MODEL

CONDITION

ESTIMATED VALUE

WHERE STORED/KEPT

ADDITIONAL COMMENTS

ITEM

DATE PURCHASED

VENDOR/STORE/DEALER

ADDRESS

PHONE #

WEB SITE/E-MAIL

ASKING PRICE   **PRICE PAID**

DESCRIPTION OF ITEM

YEAR ITEM WAS MADE

MANUFACTURER/ARTIST

MAKE/MODEL

CONDITION

ESTIMATED VALUE

WHERE STORED/KEPT

ADDITIONAL COMMENTS

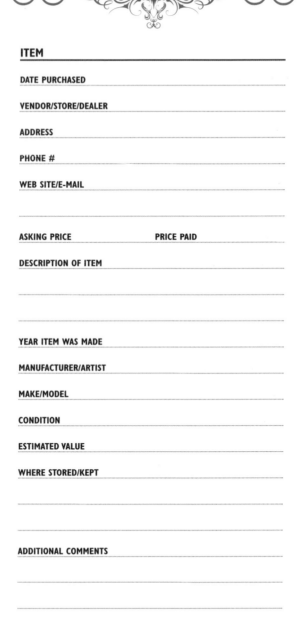

ITEM

DATE PURCHASED

VENDOR/STORE/DEALER

ADDRESS

PHONE #

WEB SITE/E-MAIL

ASKING PRICE   **PRICE PAID**

DESCRIPTION OF ITEM

YEAR ITEM WAS MADE

MANUFACTURER/ARTIST

MAKE/MODEL

CONDITION

ESTIMATED VALUE

WHERE STORED/KEPT

ADDITIONAL COMMENTS

ITEM

DATE PURCHASED

VENDOR/STORE/DEALER

ADDRESS

PHONE #

WEB SITE/E-MAIL

ASKING PRICE   **PRICE PAID**

DESCRIPTION OF ITEM

YEAR ITEM WAS MADE

MANUFACTURER/ARTIST

MAKE/MODEL

CONDITION

ESTIMATED VALUE

WHERE STORED/KEPT

ADDITIONAL COMMENTS

ITEM

DATE PURCHASED

VENDOR/STORE/DEALER

ADDRESS

PHONE #

WEB SITE/E-MAIL

ASKING PRICE   **PRICE PAID**

DESCRIPTION OF ITEM

YEAR ITEM WAS MADE

MANUFACTURER/ARTIST

MAKE/MODEL

CONDITION

ESTIMATED VALUE

WHERE STORED/KEPT

ADDITIONAL COMMENTS

ITEM

DATE PURCHASED

VENDOR/STORE/DEALER

ADDRESS

PHONE #

WEB SITE/E-MAIL

ASKING PRICE　　　　　　　**PRICE PAID**

DESCRIPTION OF ITEM

YEAR ITEM WAS MADE

MANUFACTURER/ARTIST

MAKE/MODEL

CONDITION

ESTIMATED VALUE

WHERE STORED/KEPT

ADDITIONAL COMMENTS

ITEM

DATE PURCHASED

VENDOR/STORE/DEALER

ADDRESS

PHONE #

WEB SITE/E-MAIL

ASKING PRICE   **PRICE PAID**

DESCRIPTION OF ITEM

YEAR ITEM WAS MADE

MANUFACTURER/ARTIST

MAKE/MODEL

CONDITION

ESTIMATED VALUE

WHERE STORED/KEPT

ADDITIONAL COMMENTS

ITEM

DATE PURCHASED

VENDOR/STORE/DEALER

ADDRESS

PHONE #

WEB SITE/E-MAIL

ASKING PRICE   PRICE PAID

DESCRIPTION OF ITEM

YEAR ITEM WAS MADE

MANUFACTURER/ARTIST

MAKE/MODEL

CONDITION

ESTIMATED VALUE

WHERE STORED/KEPT

ADDITIONAL COMMENTS

ITEM

DATE PURCHASED

VENDOR/STORE/DEALER

ADDRESS

PHONE #

WEB SITE/E-MAIL

ASKING PRICE   **PRICE PAID**

DESCRIPTION OF ITEM

YEAR ITEM WAS MADE

MANUFACTURER/ARTIST

MAKE/MODEL

CONDITION

ESTIMATED VALUE

WHERE STORED/KEPT

ADDITIONAL COMMENTS

ITEM

DATE PURCHASED

VENDOR/STORE/DEALER

ADDRESS

PHONE #

WEB SITE/E-MAIL

ASKING PRICE   **PRICE PAID**

DESCRIPTION OF ITEM

YEAR ITEM WAS MADE

MANUFACTURER/ARTIST

MAKE/MODEL

CONDITION

ESTIMATED VALUE

WHERE STORED/KEPT

ADDITIONAL COMMENTS

ITEM

DATE PURCHASED

VENDOR/STORE/DEALER

ADDRESS

PHONE #

WEB SITE/E-MAIL

ASKING PRICE   **PRICE PAID**

DESCRIPTION OF ITEM

YEAR ITEM WAS MADE

MANUFACTURER/ARTIST

MAKE/MODEL

CONDITION

ESTIMATED VALUE

WHERE STORED/KEPT

ADDITIONAL COMMENTS

ITEM

DATE PURCHASED

VENDOR/STORE/DEALER

ADDRESS

PHONE #

WEB SITE/E-MAIL

ASKING PRICE   **PRICE PAID**

DESCRIPTION OF ITEM

YEAR ITEM WAS MADE

MANUFACTURER/ARTIST

MAKE/MODEL

CONDITION

ESTIMATED VALUE

WHERE STORED/KEPT

ADDITIONAL COMMENTS

ITEM

DATE PURCHASED

VENDOR/STORE/DEALER

ADDRESS

PHONE #

WEB SITE/E-MAIL

ASKING PRICE   **PRICE PAID**

DESCRIPTION OF ITEM

YEAR ITEM WAS MADE

MANUFACTURER/ARTIST

MAKE/MODEL

CONDITION

ESTIMATED VALUE

WHERE STORED/KEPT

ADDITIONAL COMMENTS

ITEM

DATE PURCHASED

VENDOR/STORE/DEALER

ADDRESS

PHONE #

WEB SITE/E-MAIL

ASKING PRICE   **PRICE PAID**

DESCRIPTION OF ITEM

YEAR ITEM WAS MADE

MANUFACTURER/ARTIST

MAKE/MODEL

CONDITION

ESTIMATED VALUE

WHERE STORED/KEPT

ADDITIONAL COMMENTS

ITEM

DATE PURCHASED

VENDOR/STORE/DEALER

ADDRESS

PHONE #

WEB SITE/E-MAIL

ASKING PRICE   **PRICE PAID**

DESCRIPTION OF ITEM

YEAR ITEM WAS MADE

MANUFACTURER/ARTIST

MAKE/MODEL

CONDITION

ESTIMATED VALUE

WHERE STORED/KEPT

ADDITIONAL COMMENTS

Collectibles Wish List

Here is where you keep a
list of treasures you want
to find and acquire.
Stay on the trail as you
build your collections.

ITEM

DESCRIPTION

WHERE SPOTTED

VENDOR/STORE/DEALER

CONTACT INFO

PRICE RANGE

NOTES

ITEM

DESCRIPTION

WHERE SPOTTED

VENDOR/STORE/DEALER

CONTACT INFO

PRICE RANGE

NOTES

ITEM

DESCRIPTION

WHERE SPOTTED

VENDOR/STORE/DEALER

CONTACT INFO

PRICE RANGE

NOTES

ITEM

DESCRIPTION

WHERE SPOTTED

VENDOR/STORE/DEALER

CONTACT INFO

PRICE RANGE

NOTES

ITEM

DESCRIPTION

WHERE SPOTTED

VENDOR/STORE/DEALER

CONTACT INFO

PRICE RANGE

NOTES

ITEM

DESCRIPTION

WHERE SPOTTED

VENDOR/STORE/DEALER

CONTACT INFO

PRICE RANGE

NOTES

ITEM

DESCRIPTION

WHERE SPOTTED

VENDOR/STORE/DEALER

CONTACT INFO

PRICE RANGE

NOTES

ITEM

DESCRIPTION

WHERE SPOTTED

VENDOR/STORE/DEALER

CONTACT INFO

PRICE RANGE

NOTES

ITEM

DESCRIPTION

WHERE SPOTTED

VENDOR/STORE/DEALER

CONTACT INFO

PRICE RANGE

NOTES

ITEM

DESCRIPTION

WHERE SPOTTED

VENDOR/STORE/DEALER

CONTACT INFO

PRICE RANGE

NOTES

ITEM

DESCRIPTION

WHERE SPOTTED

VENDOR/STORE/DEALER

CONTACT INFO

PRICE RANGE

NOTES

ITEM

DESCRIPTION

WHERE SPOTTED

VENDOR/STORE/DEALER

CONTACT INFO

PRICE RANGE

NOTES

ITEM

DESCRIPTION

WHERE SPOTTED

VENDOR/STORE/DEALER

CONTACT INFO

PRICE RANGE

NOTES

ITEM

DESCRIPTION

WHERE SPOTTED

VENDOR/STORE/DEALER

CONTACT INFO

PRICE RANGE

NOTES

ITEM

DESCRIPTION

WHERE SPOTTED

VENDOR/STORE/DEALER

CONTACT INFO

PRICE RANGE

NOTES

ITEM

DESCRIPTION

WHERE SPOTTED

VENDOR/STORE/DEALER

CONTACT INFO

PRICE RANGE

NOTES

ITEM

DESCRIPTION

WHERE SPOTTED

VENDOR/STORE/DEALER

CONTACT INFO

PRICE RANGE

NOTES

ITEM

DESCRIPTION

WHERE SPOTTED

VENDOR/STORE/DEALER

CONTACT INFO

PRICE RANGE

NOTES

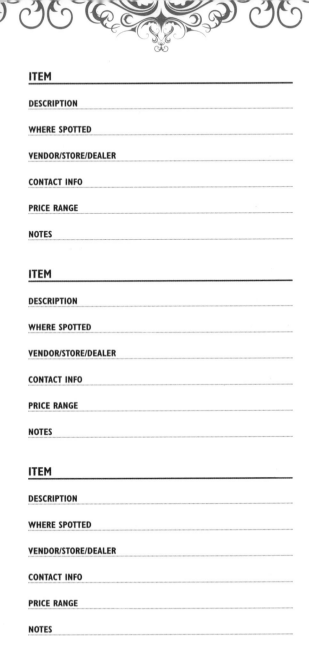

ITEM

DESCRIPTION

WHERE SPOTTED

VENDOR/STORE/DEALER

CONTACT INFO

PRICE RANGE

NOTES

ITEM

DESCRIPTION

WHERE SPOTTED

VENDOR/STORE/DEALER

CONTACT INFO

PRICE RANGE

NOTES

ITEM

DESCRIPTION

WHERE SPOTTED

VENDOR/STORE/DEALER

CONTACT INFO

PRICE RANGE

NOTES

ITEM

DESCRIPTION

WHERE SPOTTED

VENDOR/STORE/DEALER

CONTACT INFO

PRICE RANGE

NOTES

ITEM

DESCRIPTION

WHERE SPOTTED

VENDOR/STORE/DEALER

CONTACT INFO

PRICE RANGE

NOTES

ITEM

DESCRIPTION

WHERE SPOTTED

VENDOR/STORE/DEALER

CONTACT INFO

PRICE RANGE

NOTES

ITEM

DESCRIPTION

WHERE SPOTTED

VENDOR/STORE/DEALER

CONTACT INFO

PRICE RANGE

NOTES

ITEM

DESCRIPTION

WHERE SPOTTED

VENDOR/STORE/DEALER

CONTACT INFO

PRICE RANGE

NOTES

ITEM

DESCRIPTION

WHERE SPOTTED

VENDOR/STORE/DEALER

CONTACT INFO

PRICE RANGE

NOTES

ITEM

DESCRIPTION

WHERE SPOTTED

VENDOR/STORE/DEALER

CONTACT INFO

PRICE RANGE

NOTES

ITEM

DESCRIPTION

WHERE SPOTTED

VENDOR/STORE/DEALER

CONTACT INFO

PRICE RANGE

NOTES

ITEM

DESCRIPTION

WHERE SPOTTED

VENDOR/STORE/DEALER

CONTACT INFO

PRICE RANGE

NOTES

ITEM

DESCRIPTION

WHERE SPOTTED

VENDOR/STORE/DEALER

CONTACT INFO

PRICE RANGE

NOTES

ITEM

DESCRIPTION

WHERE SPOTTED

VENDOR/STORE/DEALER

CONTACT INFO

PRICE RANGE

NOTES

ITEM

DESCRIPTION

WHERE SPOTTED

VENDOR/STORE/DEALER

CONTACT INFO

PRICE RANGE

NOTES

ITEM

DESCRIPTION

WHERE SPOTTED

VENDOR/STORE/DEALER

CONTACT INFO

PRICE RANGE

NOTES

ITEM

DESCRIPTION

WHERE SPOTTED

VENDOR/STORE/DEALER

CONTACT INFO

PRICE RANGE

NOTES

ITEM

DESCRIPTION

WHERE SPOTTED

VENDOR/STORE/DEALER

CONTACT INFO

PRICE RANGE

NOTES

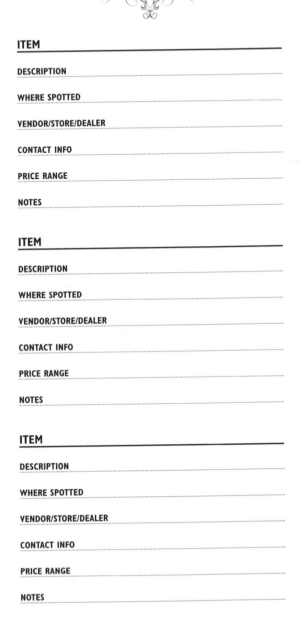

ITEM

DESCRIPTION

WHERE SPOTTED

VENDOR/STORE/DEALER

CONTACT INFO

PRICE RANGE

NOTES

ITEM

DESCRIPTION

WHERE SPOTTED

VENDOR/STORE/DEALER

CONTACT INFO

PRICE RANGE

NOTES

ITEM

DESCRIPTION

WHERE SPOTTED

VENDOR/STORE/DEALER

CONTACT INFO

PRICE RANGE

NOTES

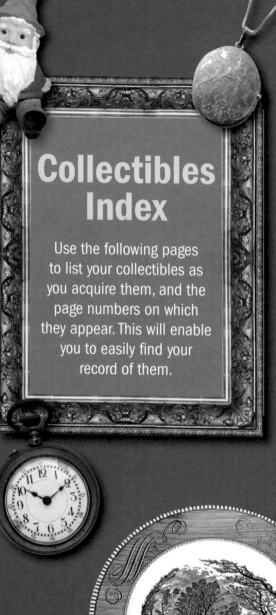

Collectibles Index

Use the following pages to list your collectibles as you acquire them, and the page numbers on which they appear. This will enable you to easily find your record of them.

Collectibles Index

ITEM	PAGE

Collectibles Index

ITEM	PAGE

Collectibles Index

ITEM	PAGE

Collectibles Index

ITEM	PAGE

Collectibles Index

ITEM	PAGE

Collectibles Index

ITEM	PAGE

Collectibles Index

ITEM	PAGE